COUNTRYSIDE
KAWARTHA

Canadian Cataloguing in Publication Data

Mallory, Enid, 1938–
    Countryside Kawartha

Includes bibliographical references.
ISBN 0-9693497-2-6

1. Kawartha Lakes Region (Ont.) - Description and
travel. 2. Kawartha Lakes Region (Ont.) - History.
 I. Title.

FC3095.K39M35 1994   917.13'67   C94-931945-7
F1059.K2M35 1994

Published by Peterborough Publishing
(a division of Mallpro Corporation)
R.R.#2, Peterborough, Ontario, K9J 6X3

Printed and bound in Canada by Friesen Printers.

Jacket front: Anderson farm near Warsaw.

Facing page: Hunter farm in Douro.

COUNTRYSIDE
KAWARTHA

ENID MALLORY

PHOTOGRAPHY: GORD AND ENID MALLORY

ACKNOWLEDGEMENTS

A colour book was also in my mind as I wrote *KAWARTHA: Living on These Lakes*. That book dealt with the people who settled around the lakes using stories and photography to tell their history. Historical photos are always black-and-white; in reality, for the people in those photos and for us here today, the Kawarthas shine in living colour. This book attempts to catch the colour.

Thanks to all those who introduced us to scenic Kawartha places, hills, valleys, lakes, creeks, side-roads; to events, festivals, celebrations. Thanks to all those who expressed feelings for a special locale, a sense of place, a spirit of community, a love of the land. Such awareness is often contagious.

Thanks to those whose farms or cottages, or hens or horses appear in this book, those who took us on sleighrides or let us walk on their farms or showed us their lake or a glimpse of their wildlife.

Among those who answered questions and helped with facts were the staff of the Peterborough Public Library, Jean Cole, Frances Douglas, Albert DeGryse, Terry Gross, Jim Patterson and Connie Wahl. Thanks to Edith Fowke for permission to quote from her *Traditional Singers and Songs from Ontario*, to McClelland and Stewart for permission to quote from Margaret Laurence's *Heart of a Stranger* and *Dance on the Earth: A Memoir*, to Natural Resources for permission to quote from Cummings, H.R., *Early Days in Haliburton*, to Friends of the Trent-Severn Waterway for permission to adapt the map from *The Trent-Severn Waterway: an Environmental Exploration*.

A special thanks to Gord for sharing this project with me, to Arlene Stephens and Peter Mallory for artistic advice, and to Jean Brien, our editor.

for Peter, Jonathan, Allison, Laurie

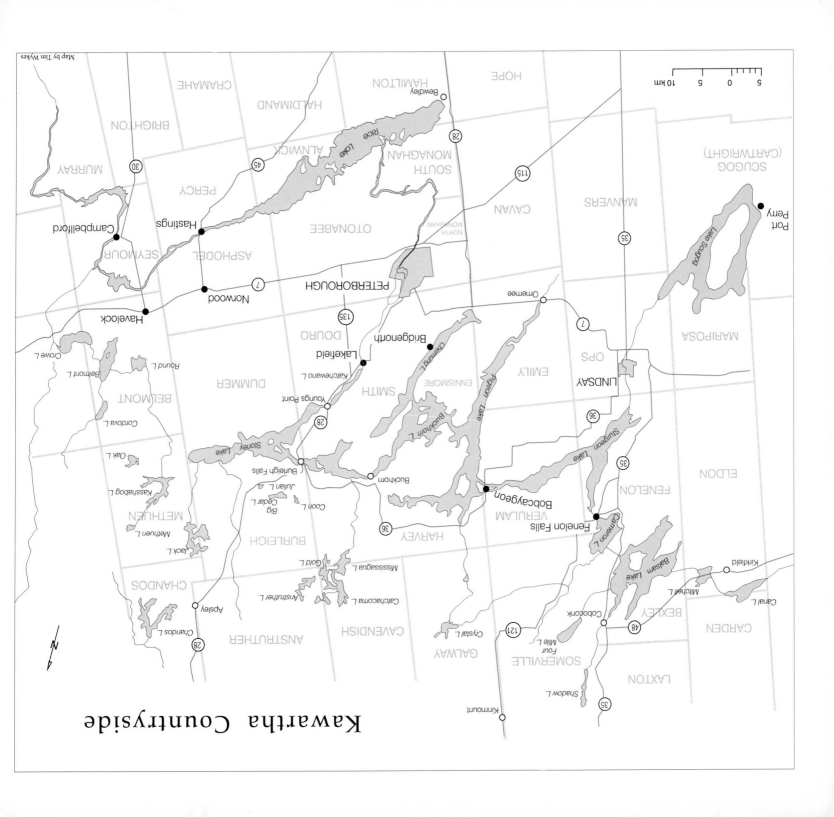

Kawartha Countryside

Sunset, Lily Lake

TABLE OF CONTENTS

Springtime garden at the Earle farm on the third line of Smith.

LIVING NEAR PRECIOUS CORNERS

There really is a Precious Corners; it lies south of Rice Lake on the edge of the Kawartha district, close to Cobourg. But I use the term for all the specific precious corners where people established themselves as they settled the area from south to north, naming their special places Garden Hill or Mount Pleasant or Millbrook or Rosedale or Somebody's Corners.

Corners are places where a north-south road intersects an east-west road. Most often the place got a name by people referring to the owner of the farm or the mill or the store – Mathers Corners, Stewart Hall, Fraserville, Downeyville, Fowlers Corners, Youngs Point, Powles Corners.

The 'crossroads' or the 'corners' was a centre in all respects of the word. An invisible circle existed around it touching or overlapping another circle which surrounded a village three or four miles away. Within that circle farm families were drawn to the village to grind grain, have horses shod, worship God, buy their harness and sugar and tea. The village grew, flourished and then shrank over the years. At some corners only the name remains, a sort of ghost centre for what went on in the circle of living around it.

For many Kawartha people today 'the corners' is a place they knew well in the past, maybe even an address they had to get away from. But the precious label sticks; the little hamlet evokes poignant memories of the people who once played a big part in their lives. It is the place where first discoveries were made, where the world was new and there was all the time of childhood to explore it.

For other people some particular corner of the Kawarthas is a recent discovery, a space they chose. They drove past the farm or the village house and turned around and came back. The house or the valley or the drumlin hills or the view across the lake grabbed them and wouldn't let go. They became country people; they chose to live on a farm or a piece of land near Somebody's Corners.

These place-names that dot the map are like stars in the night sky pinning the countryside into some sort of pattern. These locales where we live or once lived or hope to live are part of our awareness of the Kawarthas even if we dwell in a downtown apartment. We drive out to Pontypool or Cottesloe or Omemee to visit Cousin Joe or Aunt Sadie or to feel a spring day or to see the big hill in autumn's finest colour. We sort out the countryside by the way it rolls from one village to the next or from village to lake or river.

This is a book about the Kawartha countryside as it exists today. But to see it clearly it is sometimes necessary to use the eyes of those who saw it first. We often get the sharpest, most astute descriptions from those who knew it least – the newcomer, the person just off the boat. He or she sees it with the emotional intensity of someone who has crossed an ocean and committed himself or herself to a new land. No bridges exist between that place and this, no need to burn them, no going back. So the skies are darker than they will ever be again, the snows heavier, the storms more frightening, but the colours are also brighter and the tiny flower never seen before is more exquisite than anything growing on the old sod.

That is why we still read Catharine Parr Traill with such a sense of identity. She is seeing it for us for the first time. And the young immigrant boy named Ernest Thompson, who would become famous as Ernest Thompson Seton, overwhelmed by his first sight of a bluebird, could be one of us today seeing our first bluebird.

There is another reason to look through those early eyes. They saw this land unspoiled, water so clear you could see every pebble on the bottom, air fresh and pure, virgin forests, birds and animals and natives in a natural balance, the like of which we will not see again. We can never move down the pristine water route used by Huron and Mohawk and Ojibway and by Samuel de Champlain in 1615. Nevertheless it helps to look at our lands with some idea of the natural balance which once existed here. It affects our priorities and expands our possibilities.

Sleighride on the Leahy farm in Douro Township

Mark's barn and the moon are aligned on this frosty morning.

Sullivan's General Store at "The Cross" has presided over life in Ennismore since the early years of this century.

General Store at Harwood on Rice Lake.

Crossroads at Millbrook with Cavan hills in background.

The cross on St. Mark's Anglican Church in Warsaw is being repaired on a cold, bright September afternoon.

Brown eggs for sale on Highway 35 near Cameron.

This dinosaur delight waits for the mail on the South Stoney Lake Road.

15

In October a coloured road on the Eleventh Line of Cavan rises like a stairway to heaven.

16

CHAPTER 1

THE HILLS OF CAVAN
(AND MANVERS AND CARTWRIGHT)

Hills are a first sign of the Kawarthas for anyone approaching from the west on Highways 7 or 115. You come over the big hill on 115 near the intersection of 35, and the open look of the Kawartha land is suddenly there, offering a sense of solidity and space, a feeling that you are firmly grounded but you can see forever. The barns, symbolic of hard work and rural bounty, are set into the drumlin hills, anchored against the winter blizzards, boasting of livestock and harvest gathered in. Horses on a hill, a herd of grazing cows, a glimpse of whitetail deer speak of a pleasant mix of order and freedom.

This land has not been dumped on by cement trucks. The past is not obliterated. If you look with even a little knowledge, the ice age is still visible.

Drumlins, appearing as you drive east, are elongated low-lying hills formed under sheets of ice when a unique balance occurred between forces of erosion and deposition. There are 4000 drumlins on the Kawartha countryside.

Eskers, which are long sinuous deposits of sand and gravel, were formed by meltwater in subglacial streams; they occurred where retreating ice halted for long periods of time. Some of the Kawartha eskers run for several kilometres. One running north and east from Bethany can be followed along the Hogs Back hiking trail 12 km to Omemee.

The Oak Ridge Interlobate Moraine is a range of hills, 160 km long and 1 to 15 km wide, sometimes rising 100 m above the base terrain. On your right as you drive east, its dunes of sand are covered by the Ganaraska Forest. The moraine was formed between two ice lobes in the final stages of the Wisconsin ice age.

Highway 115 takes you up and down on a landscape where the ice-age played havoc. Grand forces frolicked here, making all the drumlins march in the same direction, south-south-west, like soldiers bent double by the weight of ice; leaving spillways that once drained glacial lakes and are now beautiful rivers connecting the upper Kawartha Lakes to Lake Scugog and Rice Lake and Lake Ontario; shaping moraines and eskers which elevate the traveller to scenic viewpoints; creating valleys and sparkling lakes.

For early natives this was a favoured place to live. George Andrew Wilson was working on his Cavan farm (Lot 7, Con. 13) in the spring of 1961 when he turned up Indian artifacts. Dr. Walter Kenyon, from the Royal Ontario Museum, brought a 10-member field party to investigate the site. Here they found a village had covered 15-20 acres. The time was 500-600 years ago. The people were Iroquois, living in log houses, growing corn and tobacco and using the wild game and fish from the rich Cavan hills and clear valley streams. In one corner of the site Kenyon's crew found a large hollowed grindstone where the people had sharpened knives and arrows and ground their flour and corn.

In the early 1800s, settlers from Ireland were quick to see good land. Hard on the heels of surveyors Samuel Wilmot and John Deyell, in 1817 they pushed in from the settled front township of Hope.

Lack of major water bodies meant that transportation was by foot, on rough trails at best, through virgin forest and swamp at worst. But the settler who stopped by the fast-flowing streams (Baxter Creek, Squirrel Creek, Trout Creek, Jackson Creek) – saw mills in his mind's eye – sawmills at first to turn forest into houses and barns, then grist mills, flour mills, oat mills and carding mills. A mill could make a few cabins in the wilderness become a self-sufficient community. The abundance of mills made lumber so plentiful that some of the grand homes of Cavan are built of 'stacked plank', solid lumber piled from foundation to roof.

As Kawartha settlement advanced, the colonial government developed a policy of scattering half-pay English army and navy officers among and between the Irish Protestants and Irish Catholics to buffer religious differences. But Cavan and Ennismore townships stand as exceptions to this rule. In the 1825 Peter Robinson emigration, Ennismore would be settled solidly by Irish Catholics. Cavan, settled eight years earlier was solidly Irish Protestant.

Perhaps the wonder is not that a little bigotry arrived here, but that so much was left behind. In general the people of the Kawarthas are a model of tolerance; they delight in each other's differences. The Cavan Blazers were the exception.

Their heyday was about 1840 to 1870 when many of them lived between Cavanville and Mount Pleasant on the 9th, 10th and 11th concessions. They were members of the Loyal Orange Lodge, young men whose exploits became notorious. The origin of the name 'Blazers' has several possibilities; one of the most plausible deals with deliberately-set fires. In the town of Cavanville, after a postmaster and druggist named John Knowlson 'turned' Roman Catholic, a small settlement of Catholics grew up around his corner. One night the cabins were burned to the ground and the settlers driven out of the township. The men suspected of torching the cabins became known as the Cavan Blazers.

The Blazers were not all bad. When ague caused farmers to sicken or die, young men who had harvested all day at home, went out again by moonlight to save the crops of sick neighbours (Protestant, of course).

Many of their exploits singled out anyone thought to be out of line: tollgate keepers who demanded money, ministers who preached too long, a man whose cow was a nuisance grazing by the church door. It was when their pranks focused on the Irish Catholic minority in the township or moved outside of Cavan to deliberately

Seen from Highway 7A,
a house sits framed by
hills and trees.

19

Ditch grasses bleached by sun and frost dance in the wind.

St. Paul's, on the Fourth Line of Cavan. In 1820 the Anglican Church recorded only two ministers between Toronto and Belleville, one in Cobourg, the other in Cavan. Settlers met in a log school until St. Paul's was built in 1837.

'take on' Catholics, that they became a menace to law and order. On the 6th Line they set fire to the house of Paddy Maguire, a devout Roman Catholic who had brought a priest from Peterborough to celebrate mass. On March 17, 1863, they marched to Peterborough to stop a St. Patrick's day parade. Mayor Charles Perry was forced to read the Riot Act to avoid armed conflict. A few years later they burned down St. Mary's church in Port Hope.

The hope of most people who live in Cavan now is that the legendary Cavan Blazers are a part of the past, their torches buried somewhere on the 9th, 10th or 11th Line like the Iroquois tomahawks on the 13th Line.

Although close to the sprawling metropolis of Toronto, Cavan's green hills provide a certain isolation and some protection for its Irish heritage. There are still roads in Cavan that peter out to trails where you can almost see a saddlebag preacher come riding out of the mist, his horse alert to the treacherous footing, his few possessions flapping against the horse's flank, his cloak pulled tight against the morning cold. You catch a glimpse of the fervor in his eye when he passes. He's a man fit to conquer both the wilderness and the devil, and you suspect from what you've seen that he enjoys both the hardship and the glory.

Saddlebag preachers were horseback missionaries sent out when the Methodist Episcopal Church from the United States established a circuit from Smith's Creek (Port Hope). It was a charge amazing in size, in hardship and in the zeal of its preachers. Rev. Anson Green tells how he and his brethren operated.

We preach in twelve townships, have thirty-three appointments each for every twenty-eight days, lead all the classes after public service, preach funeral sermons, and attend as many prayer meetings as possible. Our Circuit embraces all the country between Bowmanville and the Carrying Place, River Trent and Mud Lake. It requires a ride of 400 miles to get round it, when we performed, winter and summer, on horseback. [1]

The strength of Methodism in Cavan is evident by their twenty churches built along the concession road (compared with five Anglican, nine Presbyterian and one Pentecostal). No Roman Catholic churches were ever built in Cavan but Roman Catholics now celebrate mass at 9 a.m. every Sunday morning in Millbrook in the sanctuary of Grace Presbyterian Church, filing out as the Presbyterians file in. The Rev. Anson Green, Paddy Maguire and the Cavan Blazers would be amazed!

Along the east edge of Manvers township about 5 km north of Bethany the ice age left a recreational delight in the Bethany ski hills. The largest hill (Silver Fox) drops 100 m in a 660 m run. Before Collingwood's Blue Mountain was developed, Toronto skiers rode the CPR en masse to Bethany. In 1939 the Ontario Downhill and Slalom Championships were held at Bethany.

Ghost villages haunt many corners of the Kawarthas. Someday if you are skiing in a snowstorm at the top of Bethany's Devil's Elbow, you might think you see a child in an old-fashioned coat carrying a slate, or a schoolmaster waving a hickory stick. The residents of the lost village of Franklin actually built their first log schoolhouse high on the top of Devil's Elbow.

The village started soon after Samuel Wilmot's 1816-17 survey of Manvers, with a mill on Fleetwood Creek, operated by Francis (Frank) Lynn. When the Midland Railway went through Franklin in 1856-57 the little town – its school still on the mountain top, its grist and saw mill very busy – had two churches, two stores, hotels, a

Lombardy poplars hold their top leaves against the autumn wind. Near Port Perry.

post office, a blacksmith shop, cattle yards and grain elevators. "Hec" Tripp remembered his grandfather's store in the early 1900s as a place where you could buy groceries, confectionery, fruits, oysters, fish, canned goods, coal oil, oil of lavender, harness, dry-goods, boots and shoes. And when you finished shopping you could skate on Grandad's rink or have a dance in the store's Hoedown room.

In 1928 the trains stopped running through Franklin. The Canadian Pacific in 1912 had run its line farther west missing Franklin. With the trains gone, the village itself began to slowly disappear.

Hillside shadows in Cavan.

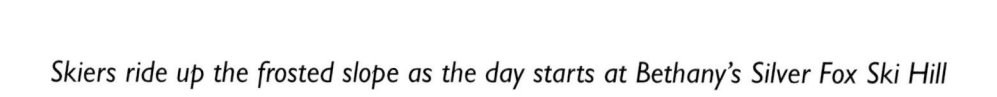

Skiers ride up the frosted slope as the day starts at Bethany's Silver Fox Ski Hill

Sap in the bucket is magic when you're not quite three. Kennedy sugar bush south of Millbrook.

25

Campbellford's buildings print their images on the Trent River.

CHAPTER 2

ARRIVALS

(HAMILTON, ALNWICK, PERCY, SEYMOUR,
SOUTH MONAGHAN, OTONABEE, ASPHODEL)

The towns along the south shore of Rice Lake have been places of great activity. People arrived here. Having made it across the ocean, up the St. Lawrence, then from Cobourg by foot or by cart, they were stopped by Rice Lake.

Rice Lake lies only 48 km north of "the front", the corridor of travel leading from Kingston to Toronto. Hamilton township had been settled early and a plank road stretched all the way to Gore's Landing by 1846. Any adventurer who came to the New World could trek to Rice Lake. Settlers who left wives and children behind in Cobourg or Port Hope, crossed the lake and went up the Otonabee. After the first shanty was built in a clearing somewhere beyond Rice Lake, they would return for their families.

People embarking at Gore's Landing used crude scows or punts or canoes at first, elegant steamboats in later years. Harwood became the scene of tremendous excitement for a few years when a railroad stretched 4 km across the lake. A world-class wonder in 1854, it succumbed to wind and ice in 1862.

Not all the arrivals crossed the lake. Hamilton, Alnwick, Percy and Seymour townships could be reached easily by settlers pushing up from the Front. The Rice Lake plains, used by the Iroquois for the growing of corn, appeared attractive and park-like to would-be settlers after a long trek through virgin forest. For many, the lake was the mecca. Its wonderful fishing and great rafts of ducks attracted young sportsmen who became old sportsmen and settled down in paradise at Gore's Landing or Harwood or somewhere along the shore. Early tourists were taking afternoon tea or whisky in civilized hotel-boarding houses beside Rice Lake while the other Kawartha Lakes remained *in puris naturalibus* with only deer and wolves sipping or nibbling along their shores.

On the lake's north shore (later to become Monaghan, Otonabee and Asphodel townships), a landscape of

On three sides of this tall monument to Joseph Scriven are the verses of his hymn, *What a Friend We Have in Jesus,* sung in every Christian country in the world.

Beside the tall Scriven monument erected in 1919 is a small stone to Eliza Catherine [Roche] and this footstone which reads, "Scriven's Sweetheart".

rolling hills offered fertile farmland once the forest was cleared. A number of retired army officers on half pay were granted large tracts of land along the water. Capt. Charles Rubidge of the Royal Navy, was the first settler in Otonabee to obtain title to his land. Lieut. Philip James Elmhirst, who served under Nelson at the Battle of the Nile and at Trafalgar, received 1000 acres along Rice Lake in the area where Elmhirst Lodge sits today.

The most famous name associated with land grants along Rice Lake was Sir Isaac Brock. After Brock died at Queenston Heights in the War of 1812, 12,000 acres were granted to Sir Isaac's four brothers, 3000 of it in Monaghan township. In 1835 the Monaghan land was settled by Captain Robert Pengelley who married Brock's niece, Harriet. Harriet died soon after arriving here and Robert later married a daughter of Capt. John Roche.

The Pengelley land is near the west end of Rice Lake on the north shore. In a small cemetery on the farm lies a man who tutored the Pengelley children, described by those who knew him as humble and kind and eccentric. Double tragedy marked the life of Joseph Scriven. Born in County Down, Ireland, in 1819, he graduated from Trinity College in Dublin. When he was 23, his bride-to-be drowned one day before they were to be married. He came to Canada in 1845 and in 1850 came to the Pengelley family as a tutor.

Catherine Roche, a niece of the Pengelleys, who often stayed with them on the farm, became his new love. When she converted to his Plymouth Brethren faith, he baptised her in the cold waters of a creek running into Rice Lake. She was 23 at the time and already showing signs of consumption. She caught a chill and died.

Scriven's response to tragedy was religious fervour expressed in a Christ-like generosity to all around him. He is remembered as a man who gave away his only coat because someone needed it more, who went around sawing and chopping wood for widows and for the old and needy.

Out of his own grief and faith he wrote the words of a hymn which a Port Hope publisher put in his newspaper. Someone used that newspaper to wrap a parcel going to New York City. There the parcel was opened, the verses read and shown to a New York newspaperman. The manager of the Burdette Organ Co. of Erie Pa., sat down and composed the music. The hymn's first line was, *What a friend we have in Jesus ...* .

To some, Joseph Scriven was strange, suspect, a man who hung around widows, who wrote poems, who prayed in public places. Twenty-six years after Catherine's death, Scriven died suddenly. A fellow Brethren was caring for him during an attack of fever. On the morning of Oct. 10, 1886, he was found in the flume of a dam near Rice Lake, his body kneeling as if in prayer.

The mystery of Scriven's death was heightened by the presence of a third man in the house that night, a young man who had been befriended by Scriven. History reveals this man to have been a criminal and possibly a lunatic. Did Scriven die of a fever, or possibly suicide, or was he murdered?

He is buried in the tiny Pengelley cemetery beside Catherine Roche whose footstone says, *Scriven's Sweetheart*. On his own large monument erected in 1920 "by lovers of his Hymn" and unveiled in a ceremony attended by an estimated 8000 people, are chiselled the four verses of his famous hymn.

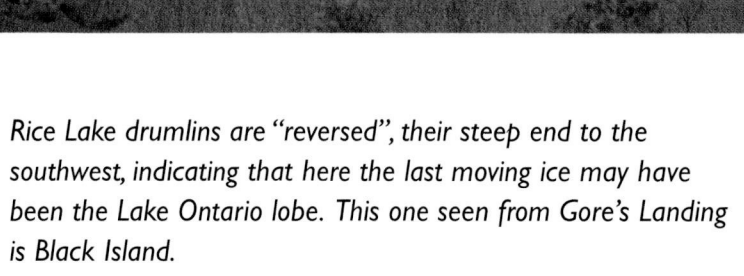

Rice Lake drumlins are "reversed", their steep end to the southwest, indicating that here the last moving ice may have been the Lake Ontario lobe. This one seen from Gore's Landing is Black Island.

Large brick houses built in the late 1800s give the Kawartha countryside a look of enduring prosperity. This one is on County Road 2 on Rice Lake's north shore.

The Rice Lake Indians appear to be more intelligent, and are the handsomest company of men I have seen. Potash (Paudash), their chief, is very majestic in appearance, possesses a commanding voice, and speaks with great animation.
Egerton Ryerson, *The Story of My Life,* 1883.]

Ryerson taught at Hiawatha in 1827, a year after Chief Paudash accepted Christianity. The Rice Lake mission, with Alderville on the south shore and Hiawatha on the north shore, became a training centre for evangelists like Peter Jones, John Sunday, Peter Jacobs, Henry Steinhauer, James Evans, George Copway, William Herkimer and Charlie Big Canoe, who spread the gospel across Canada.

The church at Hiawatha.

The history of the Ojibway like that of other Indian tribes is treasured up in traditional lore. It has been passed down from age to age on the tide of song, for there is much poetry in the narrative of the old sage as he dispenses his facts and fancies to the listening group that throng around him.

Kah-ge-ga-gah-bowh, *Traditional History and Characteristic Sketches of the Ojibway Nation, 1851*[2]

Pow-wow at Curve Lake

Kah-ge-ga-gah-bowh, also known as George Copway, was born in 1818 near Trenton and brought up in the woods. The Methodist missionary school at Rice Lake launched him into the white man's world. He became an interpreter, school teacher, ordained minister, missionary and world traveller, and the first native Indian to write a book.

In 1840 he married Elizabeth Howell, daughter of an English officer, in Toronto. Elizabeth suffered cold, hunger and hardship when she shared his missionary travels in the Lake Superior wilderness. Copway's own endurance became legendary when he travelled 185 miles on foot to return in two days with food for starving friends.

He went on to lecture in the United States, England and Europe, and to edit a newspaper. In 1847 his book, *History and Travels of Kahgegagahbowh,* was published. His narrative poem, *Ojibway Conquest,* appeared in 1850, a year after he became a friend of Henry Wadsworth Longfellow. *Traditional History and Characteristic Sketches of the Ojibway Nation* was published in 1851.

In spite of remarkable ability and a dynamic personality, Copway found the leap from Ojibway world to white man's world too great. Money problems, family problems and spiritual uncertainty beset him. Accused of embezzling funds, he was expelled from the Methodist church. Just before he died he became a convert to Roman Catholicism.

33

Two visitors to Hastings watch houseboats
move upstream on a summer morning.

Dorette Carter pauses on a winter
walk at Lang Century Village.

*North Monaghan barn
near Springville.*

*Rare wooden silo on the Noddle
farm, County Road 2 near Rice Lake.*

A rainbow appears in the spray beneath Healey Falls, situated above the junction of the Crowe River with the Trent.

Richard Bonnycastle served in the War of 1812. In the rebellion of 1837 he commanded the Kingston garrison. For this service he was knighted and made commander, Royal Engineers, for Upper Canada from 1837 to 1839. Whenever possible he travelled through the countryside viewing public works and recording his impressions which he published in two books: *The Canadas in 1841* and *Canada and the Canadians.*

His son, Henry, had settled in Seymour township in 1826. To visit him and see the Rice Lake area in 1845 Sir Richard journeyed by wagon over roots and stumps and stones "as big as bombshells", wishing the proposed Trent Canal were already built. The dam and two timber slides at Healey's Falls had just been constructed the year before and Sir Richard was anxious to see them. Healey Falls almost cost him his life.

A vast timber canal or way had been constructed here by the Board of Works to convey timber down a rapid without danger, the slide being alongside of that rapid. It was an interesting work; and with my young friend and two naval officers, settled in Seymour, I went to examine it. At the sluiceway or timber-dam was a sort of bridge composed of parallel pieces of heavy square joists and a platform ...

The parallel pieces were about two feet distant from each other; I walked on one and my companion on the other, until a good view of the whole work and the splendid rapids was attained. Under our feet at some distance was the water of the slide running on an inclined plane of woodwork, at a great angle and with enormous power and velocity into a pitch or cauldron far below.

The day was bright, and the shadow of the parallel logs left between the space no view of the water underneath. They called me suddenly to look at the rapid; I jumped, as I thought over the space between us; but my jump was into the shadow. One of the naval officers, a powerful man six feet and more in height, saw me jump; and just as I was disappearing between the timbers caught me by the arm and by sheer muscle and strength, held me in midair. The other immediately assisted him, but my young friend became deadly pale and sick. I did not visit either the slide or the cauldron; in either, instantaneous and suffocating death was inevitable. Reader, never leap in dark places, and look before you leap.

Sir Richard Bonnycastle, *Canada and the Canadians,* 1849.[3]

In a powerful surge of sound and light, Healey Falls plunges 23 m over a limestone cliff that is 143 m wide.

The Fountain in
Little Lake.

CHAPTER 3

NOGOJIWANONG
(PLACE AT THE END OF THE RAPIDS – PETERBOROUGH)

The camping place at the end of the rapids – Nogojiwanong, the Ojibway called it – is now covered by a city of 68,000. But the good bones of the countryside show through. Hills and parks wear their trees and shrubs and flowers well. The Otonabee River courses through the city and the Trent-Severn Waterway carries boat traffic into a little lake in the heart of the downtown area.

The Otonabee River has been all-important in the geography and history of Peterborough. Sometime between 12 and 10,000 years ago, the scraping of the ice age and the erosional effects of its meltwaters left an approximation of the lakes, rivers and swamps we see today. The lakes we call "The Kawarthas" were drained by spillways which became the Indian and Otonabee Rivers flowing into Rice Lake and Lake Iroquois. Where the Otonabee runs out of Lake Katchewanooka a series of rapids dropped the water 100 feet in 14 km. Where the wild waters settled to a quiet river and a little lake (a remnant of glacial Lake Peterborough), there was

Nogojiwanong, a good place to camp before starting the long portage to Chemong Lake.

There is evidence of people using the waterway as a trade route as far back as 9000 BC. In the early 1700s Ojibway Indians ousted the Iroquois from this area. One of the decisive battles was fought at the foot of the rapids on a site overlooking Little Lake.

In 1819 Adam Scott built a grist mill where a stream spilled into the small lake. Richard Birdsall surveyed the town site in 1825, and that same year 2000 Irish were brought out by Peter Robinson, commissioner of Crown lands. In 1826 the new village was named Peterborough.

Action on the river has always enlivened the town or city of Peterborough. Birch bark canoes propelled by Ojibway people inspired a board-and-batten craft known as the Peterborough canoe which made the city famous in the world of water transportation. Meanwhile lumbermen propelled giant rafts of timber down the waterway, breaking them up so the individual logs could

Since 1889 this clock tower has presided over the accomplishments and antics of Peterborough people.

run the rapids to the mills at Nassau where Trent University now stands or at Peterborough. Logs not intended for local mills would go on to Lake Ontario to be rafted again to Quebec City destined to become masts for the British navy.

Toward the end of the 19th century the building of dams and locks on the river – part of a dream called the Trent Canal – produced a supply of hydroelectric power unmatched anywhere in Ontario, which quickly drew manufacturing to Peterborough. The arrival of Edison Electric (Canadian General Electric) in 1890 was followed by the American Cereal Company (Quaker Oats) in 1901 and a dozen smaller companies. Both the Peterborough Canoe Company and the Canadian Canoe Company were thriving industries at the turn of the century. The completion of the Peterborough Lift Lock in 1904 brought international fame and a new pride to the city. The lift lock was the highest in the world.

The completion of the Trent-Severn Waterway from Lake Ontario to Georgian Bay in 1920 came too late for great commercial importance as the new Welland canal allowed grain to move through the Great Lakes instead. For a time steamboats flourished on the lakes and rivers as tourists discovered the joys of resort and cottage life. As good highways ended the heyday of the steamboat, the waterway became a route for pleasure boats. Today Parks Canada locks through thousands of boats every summer, and the city built at Nogojiwanong celebrates with a summer-long festival on the little lake.

The Quaker Oats Company which came to Peterborough in 1901 still wafts the toasty smell of cereal along the Otonabee.

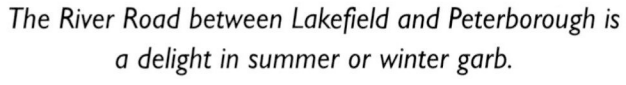

The River Road between Lakefield and Peterborough is a delight in summer or winter garb.

and look up quickly to see the magnificent unhurried sweep of those powerful wings. Margaret Laurence, *Heart of a Stranger*, 1976.[1]

Margaret Laurence came to Peterborough as writer-in-residence at Trent University, then moved to a cabin on the Otonabee River before buying a house in Lakefield. The town she made famous in *The Diviners* (1974) has been identified as Neepawa, Manitoba, but the place where she sat writing, bringing Morag and Christie to life, was on the Otonabee near Stewart Hall.

In *The Diviners* she wrote of the river that flows both ways. In her memoirs she says, *The river flowing both ways was, of course, the Otonabee River, and every time I looked up from the page I was writing at the shack, I could see it.*[2]

A blue heron stalks along the river.

My best place at the moment ... is a small cedar cabin on the Otonabee River in southern Ontario. I've lived three summers there, writing, bird-watching, river-watching...

Before sunup, I'm wakened by birdvoices and, I may say, birdfeet clattering and thumping on the cabin roof. Cursing only slightly, I get up temporarily, for the pre-dawn ritual of lighting a small fire in the old black woodstove (mornings are chilly here, even in summer) and looking out at the early river. The waters have a lovely spooky quality at this hour, entirely mist-covered, a secret meeting of river and sky. ...

A pair of great blue herons have their huge unwieldy nest about half a mile upriver, and although they are very shy, occasionally through the open door I hear a sudden approaching rush of air (yes, you can hear it)

42

Guns flash as part of a military tattoo at the Peterborough Lift Lock.

Hutchison House, now a lively museum, was built in 1837 by the citizens of Peterborough for their doctor at a cash cost of $224.

The Peterborough Lift Lock which opened in 1904 lifts boats 20 m and releases them into a higher level of the Trent-Severn Waterway.

Facing page – Illuminated boats waltz over the water to the music of the Festival of Lights during July and August.

The Greenwing Trout derby has become a rite of spring attracting 10,000 visitors each year. Only children under 15 are allowed to fish for the 4000 rainbow trout released into the short section of canal below the lift lock.

*Rowers on the Otonabee
at Trent University.*

Summer over, the ISLAND PRINCESS shimmers with a first coating of winter's ice.

The Burleigh Falls are well worth seeing ... viewed from Stony Lake, the landscape is one of remarkable beauty. The four cascades foaming and tumbling into the bay through the lofty walls of granite, overarched by the rich foliage of the dwarf oak, the more lofty pine, and the gnarled branches of the red cedar, whose roots are seen firmly fixed in the deep fissures of the overhanging rocks, present a picture whose varied features are not easily described.

Sam Strickland, *Twenty Seven Years in Canada West*, 1853.[1]

Burleigh Falls, famous beauty spot of the Kawarthas.

CHAPTER 4

FIELDS BETWEEN THE LAKES
(SMITH, ENNISMORE AND EMILY)

The Kawartha Lakes stretch long water fingers from northeast to southwest. Between the lakes lie favoured lands, fertile fields for tilling, pleasant townships in which to live. Smith township is bordered by Clear, Katchawanooka and the Otonabee on its east side, by Chemong Lake on its west, with Deer Bay and Lower Buckhorn framing the top. Ennismore is tucked between Chemong and Pigeon with Buckhorn at the top. Emily fits around the end of Pigeon Lake, touches Chemong Lake on the east and reaches half-way up the northwest side of Pigeon.

For the people who settled these spaces, water has been almost as important as land, providing fish for the supper table, ready transportation, log-driving jobs, tugboat commerce and work on locks and dams and steamboats. Recreation and scenic beauty has been taken for granted. Tragic accidents in the water or through thin ice were the dark other side of the magical waterways.

The land itself was good to the men who ploughed it. The huge, brightly painted barns of Ennismore were built by families who arrived penniless from potato famine in Ireland. They saw the riches of soil and water, pronounced the land 'holy' and wasted no time before adding industry and enthusiasm to this gift from the Blessed Mother.

Smith township, with no less than 28 concessions, reaches 28 km north from Peterborough to Buckhorn and Burleigh Falls. Good rich loam lies in its southern concessions. Surveyors working in the northern parts spoke of poor and stony areas and corners that were "nothing but rocks". These acres of nothing but rocks have found their way into hearts and pocketbooks as prized cottage lands, valued not only by Kawartha residents but by summer people from Toronto or Oakville or London.

Settlement in Smith began near Nogojiwanong even before the 1825 arrival of the Peter Robinson group. In

1818 a ship sailed from England carrying 110 Cumberland emigrants while Samuel Wilmot was surveying the township. It was autumn when they arrived; to survive the first winter they built a communal house at the junction of today's Chemong Road and Parkhill Road.

A map of Smith township looks odd. While its 28 concessions run east-west between the Otonabee River, Katchewanooka and Clear Lakes on the east and Chemong Lake on the west, the pattern is broken by three lines running north from Peterborough to Chemong Lake. The centre line is the old Indian portage in use for centuries. Samuel Wilmot used it too; on each side of it he laid out 12 lots and here he located the Cumberland settlers, giving them the benefit of a much-used trail. On Wilmot's map the trail was called "Street of Communication", later it became Communication Road, then Chemong Road. The roads which flank it on either side are known as West Communication Road and East Communication Road.

The parcel of land which became Ennismore had been withheld from settlers, the government hoping to sell it at higher prices to gentlemen interested in hunting and fishing estates. But in 1825 it was hurriedly opened to accommodate some of the 2000 Irish Catholics arriving in the assisted Peter Robinson emigration. The easiest way to bring the 67 families into Ennismore was along Wilmot's Street of Communication to the shores of Chemong Lake and across it by scow.

Once across the water the Irish settlers blessed their "holy land" and established a little bit of Ireland. With water on three sides they depended on themselves, their customs of work, their own rituals of life and death,

their closeness to the church, their love of music and entertainment – and sometimes the bottle. Their soft-spoken wit, their ability to tell a good story and to laugh at adversity is evident even today.

Eventually they built floating bridges to connect themselves with the road to Peterborough, and in 1949 the last of the Chemong floating bridges – beloved and hated and feared – was replaced by a causeway, letting in the 'other people' – cottagers and commuters who worked in town.

Emily Township was settled in two parts. A small group reached Pigeon Creek at the south end of Pigeon Lake in 1820 and bridged the creek by felling an oak tree from each side, thus marking the site which would become Omemee. The southern part of the township would be settled mostly by Irish Protestants. In 1825, one-third of the Peter Robinson immigrants would be settled on the northern concessions of Emily. These 142 families, all Roman Catholic, found good farmlands and developed strong communities around crossroads like Downeyville and Fox's Corners.

In townships bounded by water, landing places were important – places where you left land to travel on by water or to reach the other side, crossing from Emily to Ennismore or Ennismore to Smith, or Smith to Douro. King's Wharf, Fee's Landing, Gannon's Narrows, Harrington Narrows, Bridgenorth, Lakefield, Youngs Point – all are places where stories hang in the air because people met each other there or embarkations began. Crude ferries carted people and goods across; early bridges were built and later collapsed. Floating bridges at Flood's on Pigeon Lake, at Gannon's Narrows between Pigeon and Buckhorn and from Ennismore to Smith at Bridgenorth drifted into legend as cows and

Opening of the pickerel season
at Gannon's Narrows.

cars and horses and pigs and people slipped from slippery surfaces on windswept swaying bridges.

In the last 50 years quiet farmlands have been enlivened by the cottages and trailers planted along the shores. Ennismore and parts of Smith and Emily have become bedroom communities for people working in Peterborough. The landing places have turned into cottage towns, dressed up and catering to the needs of vacationers, their scenic beauty valued by the public and protected by cottage associations, township councils and volunteer organizations like the Peterborough Field Naturalists and Friends of the Trent-Severn Waterway.

Country lane between Bridgenorth and Lakefield.

Summer visitors to the Kawarthas fish, swim and holiday at cottages like these at Youngs Point.

Dandelions on the lane to the barn in
soft spring light. Chemong Road.

Horses on Lily Lake Road.

Dark fences frame white fields near Bridgenorth.

Cows in the mist.

Herefords graze beside the Norris farm.

Lockington farmhouse in the strong light of late afternoon.

Feeding time for Smith Township hens.

Corn caught in early snow on the Third Line of Smith.

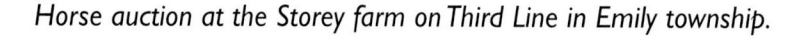

Horse auction at the Storey farm on Third Line in Emily township.

*Barn reflected in
pond on the Second
Line of Smith.*

The old bridge at Youngs Point, and the irrestible urge to jump off.

Mr. Kawartha Canoe Head.

The end of Chemong Lake near Fowlers Corners.

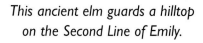

*This ancient elm guards a hilltop
on the Second Line of Emily.*

Cows pose beside a log barn on the 7th Line of Douro.

CHAPTER 5

STONES AND SONGS
(DOURO AND DUMMER)

When the 2000 Irish of the Peter Robinson immigration camped on the plains west of the Otonabee in 1825, two households were already established on the east bank in Douro township. The families of Robert Reid and Thomas Stewart were delighted to have 60 Irish families cross the river and take up land in the southern half of Douro. Sam Strickland, who married Reid's daughter, Mary, followed the river 6 km northeast to establish the village of Lakefield in 1831. A year later his sister, Catharine Parr Traill and her husband, Thomas, arrived, and then another sister, Susanna, and her husband, J. Dunbar Moodie.

The literary output of the Strickland-Traill-Moodie family – letters home, magazine articles, poetry and books – gives us an unparalleled view of pioneer lives; they also give us delightful Douro characters who would have been completely lost to posterity had they not been ensnared by those busy pens. One such personality, captured by Dunbar Moodie, is the "Ould Dhragoon"

who fixed his abode on the verge of an extensive beaver meadow.

... I encountered the old man, attired in an old hood or bonnet of his wife Judy's, with his patched canvass trowsers rolled up to his knees; one foot bare, and the other furnished with an old boot, which from its appearance had once belonged to some more aristocratic foot. His person was long, straight, and sinewy, and there was a light springiness and elasticity in his step which would have suited a younger man, as he skipped along with a handspike over his shoulder.

Off then we went, with the 'Ould Dhragoon' skipping and bounding on before us over fallen trees and mossy rocks, now ducking under the low tangled branches of the white cedar, then carefully piloting us along rotten logs covered with green moss, to save us from the discomfort of wet feet. All this time he still kept one of his feet safely ensconced in the boot while the other seemed to luxuriate in the water, as if there were something amphibious in his nature...

Beaver meadow.

When we had obtained firm footing on the opposite side we sat down to rest ourselves before commencing the operation of 'blazing', or marking the trees with our axes, along the side-line of my lot. Here the mystery of the boot was explained. Simpson very coolly took it off from the hitherto favored foot, and drew it upon the other. He was not a bit ashamed of his poverty, and candidly owned that this was the only boot he possessed, and he was desirous of giving each of his feet fair play.[1]

After supper Judy begged him to sing for Dunbar the song he made up when he first came to Canada. Two verses of Dan Simpson's song aptly describe the place where he and Judy lived.

I live on the banks of a meadow,
Now see that my maning you take;
It bates all the bogs of ould Ireland -
Six months in the year it's a lake.

Bad luck to the beavers that dammed it,
I wish them all kilt for their pains;
For shure though the craters are clever,
'Tis sartin they've droen'd my domains.[1]

Dan Simpson's song recorded by Moodie sometime before 1866 symbolizes a Douro tradition of folk singing that reaches back to Ireland and encompasses present day musical groups such as Tanglefoot which features Douro songs on their latest compact disk.

Social life has revolved around the church since early days in Douro. Musical entertainment at church socials, picnics, family reunions, weddings and community get-togethers featured step-dancing, old-time fiddle music and the singing of old Irish songs. Before long Douro had musical families – Sullivans, Clearys, Quinlans, Leahys – passing down their talent from one generation to another.

Tommy Sullivan made his first violin from a cigar box and thread, then discovered that hair from the horse's tail worked better. Tommy Sullivan's Hornpipe became a Douro favourite.

When folklorist, Edith Fowke, set out in 1956 to see if Ontario had songs worth recording, she had "no high hopes". This changed when the first person to sing for her was Mary (Cleary) Towns at the Towns General Store in Douro. She soon discovered that she had "...struck a very rich lode."[2]

In 1961 Edith Fowke took Mary and two other local singers to a Folk Music Conference at Laval University in Quebec City. Mary describes the occasion as "one of the highlights of my life." She had learned at an early age to lilt the songs which were passed down orally and had no written music. She and her father sang together as far back as Mary can remember. "He had a repertoire of at least 60 songs. The only instrument he played was the bones."

Most amazing of Douro's home-grown musical talent is the group known as The Leahy Family. Eleven sisters and brothers perform in concerts which include step-dancing, singing and fiddling. It all started with a father's passion for traditional Irish music, a musical mother and children who learned to sing and dance before they learned to talk. Much of their lives are now spent on tour in the United States or Ireland or Germany or somewhere in Canada, sharing the music that came out of their farmhouse kitchen and the town hall in Douro.

On a Saturday night in Douro you may still find the town hall jumping with fiddle music. The crowd on the floor does line dancing and square dancing. The musicians on stage change every hour or so as more people come through the door carrying violins. It's the Douro Olde Tyme Fiddlers group in action.

At the end of summer there is a special Labor Day event called Douro Doings , a tradition which goes back to 1923 when it was known as the Douro Church Social. Softball and horseshoe tournaments, a bicycle race, tug-o'-war, and a frog race are followed by a turkey supper and of course, stage entertainment and lots of music.

Dummer lies east of Douro and reaches north to include the entire southeast shore of Stoney Lake. Irish and English Protestants settled in 1831-'32 along the south edge of the township. The map still has few roads in the northern part.

Dummer settlers did not have an easy row to hoe. As Milt Clysdale, who grew up at Warsaw used to say, "Dummer had stone orchards and wooden houses." This was not quite accurate because his great-uncle "Blind" John Clysdale was a stone mason who helped build many beautiful stone houses in Dummer.

Stone orchards was a fairly accurate description. A lot of backs were bent and crippled by stone-picking before the stones got moved to neat stone fence rows or stone piles or to the foundations of stout Dummer barns. Today a neat patchwork of tilled fields framed in stone can be seen from the Warsaw Road as it runs along the top of the Warsaw esker.

The Warsaw Road is a forced road angled across concession lines to the mill site on the Indian River, which is the village of Warsaw. Upsteam from the village, the Warsaw Caves are an open notebook of geologic history. About 10 000 years ago a mighty river connecting glacial Lake Algonquin to glacial Lake Iroquois surged through to create a deep valley. The river also created caves and potholes in the limestone bedrock. The potholes were formed when granite debris was swirled around in whirlpools wearing bowl-shaped depressions into the limestone. The largest caves are

The biggest pothole or kettle at the Warsaw Caves, seen from above.

The kettle seen from below.

about 300 m long. There are many small potholes and four 'kettles', one 4.5 m deep and 2 m across the top.

A canoe trip up the Indian River is a strange experience. As you near the caves, you come around a bend and the river ends, cut off in front of you. You look to left or right for a channel and find none – the river has gone underground.

The stones of Dummer echo the sound of music, too. Dummer Protestants may have come to music less easily than their Roman Catholic neighbours in Douro, but no less enthusiastically. Dr. Donald Munroe who grew up in Essex county tells how his parents frowned on music: *They were afraid of what they called sprees meaning dubious company I might fall into if I ever became a fiddler at dances.*[3]

But during the first world war as a young doctor in Warsaw, Donald Munroe organized concerts raising

Limestone and sumach make a natural garden along the Indian River.

money to send care packages to the boys overseas. At first they would hire orchestras from Peterborough but that was costing too much.

We decided that if we were going to make any money for our soldiers we'd have to cut out expense. We got the council to let us use the town hall free. Arthur Choate and some of us formed our own orchestra. He played the bass viol, Hal Choate the coronet. I was first violin, and we had several others. In our first winter we raised nearly $1 200, and we spent it all on smokes and other gifts for our own Warsaw men overseas.[3]

Beatrice Selkirk married Hal, the coronet player. *His grandfather, Thomas Choate, had come from Warsaw, New York, to run a mill for Zaccheus Burnham. He built the store, too. But I think he was fonder of his singing classes than of the mill or store. He had his singing classes up over the store where we lived.*

If the living was sometimes hard, people in Douro and Dummer knew how to brighten a winter evening or celebrate the cool of a summer night with music. A Warsaw soiree or a Douro Doings was something you could look forward to when you were loading stones onto a stone-boat in the back forty.

Fence mending in early spring

Horse-power is making a comeback in the Kawarthas with powerful Belgians like these on the Drain farm near Stoney Lake. The horses are good in marshy areas, can climb rocky hills and are easy on the environment.

Marsh marigolds
erupt in sunny colour
where a stream has
drained low land.

Reydon Manor in Lakefield was built in the late 1850s by Robert Strickland near the home of his father, Sam, who founded the town.

They sleep in many a lonely spot,
Where the mighty forests grow,
Where the giant pine and stately oak
Their darkling shadows throw.
The mossy stone, or simple cross,
Its silent record keeps,
Where mouldering in the forest-shade,
The lonely exile sleeps.

From Catharine Parr Traill's *Scottish Emigrants' Song*.[4]

Catharine Parr Traill's grave is in the little Hillside Cemetery at Lakefield.

Many of the singers I have recorded live in and around Peterborough. Although I have since sampled many other parts of the province, no other has proved so rich in singers and songs. It is far enough away from the main industrial centers to have kept some of its early pioneer atmosphere, and many of the people living there today are descendants of the original Irish settlers who came out in 1825. ... On the rural roads and in the little villages around it live many people whose forefathers carved farms out of the wilderness early in the nineteenthy century.
Edith Fowke, *Traditional Singers and Songs From Ontario, 1965.*[5]

Fiddle music and folk songs express the Irish heritage of many Kawartha people.

Hay bales balance on a drumlin against the sky, on Peterborough County Road 38.

Towns' store at Douro has survived for more than a century.
In 1992 the Towns family staged a grand celebration to
thank their customers for 100 years of loyalty.

Water moves swiftly down from Jack Lake to Little Jack Lake.

CHAPTER 6

BIG ORE BODIES AND VEINS OF GOLD
(BELMONT, METHUEN AND CHANDOS)

One of the first settlers in Belmont, a Mr. Feddick, was driven out by the constant howling of the wolves. He reportedly gave up his land grant and moved out to Keeler's Mills (Norwood) about 1842.

Farther east in Belmont the loneliness along the Crowe River was disturbed soon after the war of 1812 by Royal Engineers in search of an overland route from Ottawa to Georgian Bay. When they found "iron and other metals," Belmont became one of the most exciting corners of the Kawarthas. A mountain of iron ore about 50 ft. from Crowe Lake attracted Charles Hayes of W & R Hayes, Dublin, Ireland. Hayes took on the job of surveying three townships and in return was granted 8534 acres in Belmont including the "great ore bed."

The ore was transported on barges five miles across Crowe Lake to the iron works which Hayes had established at Marmora. Each trip took two days. By the 1850s such slow transportation made the operation unprofitable and promoters and politicians clamoured

for a railroad. In 1867 the Cobourg, Peterborough and Marmora Railway and Mining Company had a line into the site, and ore started moving in a new direction, to the little hamlet of Trent River. There it was moved by steamer and barge to Harwood on Rice Lake (the railroad bridge across Rice Lake had crumbled in 1861). From Harwood, the ore was put on rails again to Cobourg where scows made three trips a day carrying it across Lake Ontario to a smelter at Rochester.

As the Fathers of Confederation were meeting, the town at the Belmont mine site, now named Blairton, had three stores, three hotels, a school, church, post office, blacksmith shop, two bake shops, liveries, a railway and a telegraph station. On Confederation Day, *The Globe* newspaper advertised for 400 workers for the mine, while English and Scottish papers carried similar ads with the bonus of free passage to Canada.

At least 300 000 tons of ore were removed from Belmont's mountain of iron ore before operations ceased in 1883, and some estimates suggest 1.8 million

Boathouse at Devils Lake near
the Blue Mountain mine .

Blue Mountain's nepheline syenite rock formation
in Methuen Township east of Stoney Lake.

tons are still untouched. Blairton, meanwhile, is only the ghost of a town.

Gold was found last summer in appreciable quantity in a quartz vein in the neighbouring township of Belmont ... . This report appearing in an 1865 directory for the County of Hastings puts the discovery of gold in Belmont 34 years before the discovery of gold in the Klondike.

In Madoc Township 25 km east of Belmont, a gold strike in 1866 resulted in the Eldorado gold rush, but nothing happened to Belmont's gold until 1890 when H.T. Strickland stopped his horse along a road in Belmont to give it a drink. The heavy rainfall, which provided water for the horse, also highlighted visible gold. "H.T." was the son of Sam Strickland of Lakefield. Along with farming, Sam and his sons were involved in every enterprise the backwoods had to offer: fishing, hunting, steamboating, canal and railroad building, lumbering and mining. "H.T." would be quick to recognize gold when he and his horse stumbled upon it. With two partners, he set about developing the gold mine later known as Belmont or Cordova, which produced 22 774 ounces from 121 000 tons of ore between 1892 and 1940, twice as much as any other mine in southeastern Ontario.

The town known as Cordova Mines enjoyed the rowdiness common to all mining towns. The story of "The Plug" is still told in the area. The Plug was an illegal and portable pub situated on the border of Peterborough and Hastings county. It could quickly be moved into Hastings County when Peterborough law officers were approaching and just as quickly moved back if there was news of Hastings police on the prowl.[1]

In Methuen Township, Blue Mountain stands 60 m above the surrounding granite, its sides shining as sunlight strikes the white igneous rock. Nepheline syenite is a rare ore useful in the manufacture of glass and ceramics. Claims were staked on Blue Mountain in 1932, and for many years Canada had a world monopoly on the production of nepheline syenite.

Ore is hauled into a mill where a magnetic separation circuit removes iron-bearing material. Rails then carry the ore to world markets. This Nephton ore body being mined by Indusmin Ltd. is the only nepheline syenite being commercially quarried in Canada.

Chandos, to the north of Methuen, had a flurry of mining activity spilling north from Belmont and neighbouring Hastings County in the 1860s. But, except for the short-lived Clydesdale mine near Lasswade, nothing came of it. Chandos settlers had to content themselves with farming supplemented in the early days by lumbering. The lake, which the Indians called "Mongosogan" and white people called "Loon", then "Chandos", proved to be the golden nugget in the centre of the township. In the 1920s, it attracted hotels and tourist resorts, and then the cottage economy which flourishes today.

Meanwhile Belmont, with small lakes like Round and Belmont and Cordova and Crowe; and Methuen, with Oak and Kasshabog and Jack Lakes, have made the same discovery – that the true gold lies in their beautiful lakes.

Autumn forest at Round Lake in Belmont township.

At Cordova Lake, ruins of a large power house and cradles for the penstock recall the gold mining days of the early 1900s. Two dams at the foot of Deer (Cordova) Lake created a reservoir from which a 1.8 m flume ran 517 m to the power house, driving two turbines which activated a large two-stage air compressor. Compressed air was then piped 4 km through the bush to Cordova Mines.

Osprey on white pine branch.

Above left: White-tailed deer.

81

The Crowe River, tumbling down from Hastings
County, has created "The Gut", a place of scenic
grandeur easily reached from Apsley.

A canoe that drifts silently along the shore provides an observatory for viewing birds and wildlife.

Loon Lake ... was originally called, by the Indians, Mongosogan; but when the white man reached it, after making his way through the forests that lay between it and civilization, it received its present name out of respect to the thousands of loons that annually repaired to these waters about the first of June for the purpose of rearing their young.
Edwin C. Guillet, *The Valley of the Trent,*1957.[2]

On an island in Stoney Lake at a cottage called The Shanty, the Buell family kept a diary, beginning in 1897. In 1920 they recorded 57 species of birds seen at The Shanty, their list providing a reference point for bird-watchers today.[3]

Robin	Loon	Myrtle Warbler
Bluebird	Canada Goose	Spotted Sandpiper
Flicker	Grt. Blue Heron	Chimney Swift
Kingbird	Herring Gull	Black-thr. Green Warbler
Bobolink	Ring-billed Gull	Whip-poor-will
Baltimore Oriole	Redstart	Widgeon
Yellow Warbler	Sharp-shinned Hawk	Red Crossbill
Chipping Sparrow	Red-tailed Hawk	Blue Jay
Song Sparrow	Cowbird	Nashville Warbler
Meadowlark	Winter Wren	Tennessee Warbler
Barn Swallow	House Wren	Blackburnian Warbler
Goldfinch	Purple Finch	Canadian Warbler
Cedar Waxwing	Nighthawk	Wilson's Warbler
Killdeer	Yellow-bellied Flycatcher	Black thr. Blue Warbler
Semipalmated Plover	Red-eyed Vireo	Black & White Warbler
Crow	Junco	Bald Eagle
Downy Woodpecker	Crested Flycatcher	Osprey
Hairy Woodpecker	Grackle	Bank Swallow
Red-winged Blackbird	Ruffed Grouse	Barn Swallow

When the waters run high in rivers like the Mississauga,
canoe trippers are out for adventure.

CHAPTER 7

ROADS ON THE SHIELD

(BURLEIGH-ANSTRUTHER, HARVEY
AND GALWAY-CAVENDISH)

Without roads until 1860 the shield country north of the lakes lay undisturbed, holding a balance long ago achieved between wild creatures – deer, bear, wolverine, fox, beaver, otter, mink – and the aboriginal people whose trails ran through the country as unobtrusively as the trail of the wolf.

In the 1800s the Mississaugas, who were semi-settled at Curve Lake (a peninsula between Chemong and Buckhorn Lakes) or at Hiawatha on Rice Lake, had family hunting grounds in shield country. Some of their names are legendary, immortalized by storytellers and by the creeks and lakes that bear their names.

Until 1860 the settlers' world stopped at the Burleigh rocks, massive granite ridges with valleys between and, in some places, great jumbles of boulders. At the Burleigh Falls, wild water raced over the boulders. There and on Eels Creek, bridges would be the first imperative as the Burleigh Settlement Road was begun.

The road was impassable four years later because of poor construction and forest fires which had burned the bridges. In September of 1864, the Peterborough County Council declared, ... *in consequence of the devastating fires in the Township of Burleigh the crossways and Bridges in the said township are totally destroyed, so as to render the roads impassable.*[1]

The following year new work began, crews built good bridges and opened 24 miles of passable road. Eventually the road would struggle on northeast through Burleigh and into Anstruther opening up a route into the rocky wilderness along which brave or foolhardy settlers attempted to farm. That some of those settlers survived is due not to the farming but to the lumbering that enlivened this area and provided work for wood-choppers, teamsters, river-drivers, keepers of halfway houses, boarding houses, hotels, and eventually, resorts.

To get supplies to the Burleigh Road in the 1870s involved three days of effort: by hired team to Youngs Point, by canoe or boat up Clear Lake, across Stoney to Julian's Landing, then by ox team or horses 4 km through the bush to the new road. This was faster than

At Petrogylph Provincial Park north of Stoney Lake these carvings, possibly 3500 years old, attract visitors from all over the world.

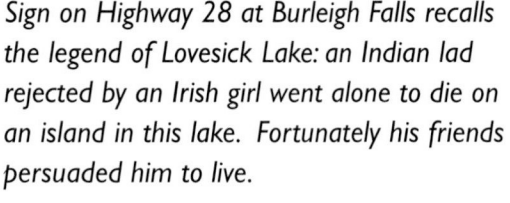

Sign on Highway 28 at Burleigh Falls recalls the legend of Lovesick Lake: an Indian lad rejected by an Irish girl went alone to die on an island in this lake. Fortunately his friends persuaded him to live.

using the road all the way. The Mount Julian Hotel, established for lumbermen in the 1870s, was a busy place with wagons and cadge teams meeting the boats and carrying supplies to the camboose shanties. The hotel still welcomes guests today, but it shares the landing site with a larger resort called Viamede.

By the 1930s the Burleigh Road was in bad shape. As a make-work effort, the government established depression camps, each with 150 men whose families were on welfare. These men rebuilt the old Burleigh Road into some semblance of a highway.

A road along the north shoreline of Stoney Lake opened only in 1975; now thousands of people come each summer to visit a site which is older than history and very special. The Peterborough Petroglyphs are rock carvings – possibly 3500 years old – on an outcropping of white crystalline limestone. Of great spiritual significance to all Native people, Petroglyphs Park has been declared a World Heritage Site. Along with the 1000 carvings, the park offers a network of trails around small lakes in the park and through the Crown Game Reserve to High Falls on Eels Creek.

In recent Kawartha history the petroglyph area was the hunting ground of a Mississauga Indian called Handsome Jack (Jack Cow). His family claimed and protected the area around Jack and Chandos Lakes, and along Eels Creek and Jack Creek.

Historians disagree on whether Jack was really handsome or remarkably ugly, but his daughter, Polly Cow, was definitely beautiful. When she died of fever, he paddled her body to an island below Youngs Point and watched by her grave night after night until he, too, died in 1835.

Lying west of Burleigh is Harvey. The largest township in all of Ontario, it has great white spaces on the map where small lakes and streams and swamps alternate with rocky ridges, where no roads go and no one lives. The south part of the township is a peninsula reaching down toward Ennismore with the waters of Buckhorn on one side and Pigeon on the other, with Big Bald and Little Bald at the top. Here, agriculture has been possible, aided and abetted by money from lumbering and water transport.

In north Harvey, lumbering meant survival. Granite ridges and valleys are interspersed with limestone flats, bare or covered with a thin overburden of soil. Rivers and small creeks run down to the lakes – Mississauga, Squaw, Nogies, Harvey. These creeks once supported vibrant lumbering communities as they carried logs to sawmills built near their mouths.

At Scott's Mill Dam on the Mississauga River one can get close to the ghosts of a lost lumbering community. A canoeist can see a 38 m concrete section, all that remains of the great timber slide that swept logs down. A hundred men worked at this mill and 30 to 40 families lived at this site before the turn of the century. From the mill, a railroad ran to Big Bald Lake where a steamboat, the Sampson No. 2, towed lumber barges or log booms down the Trent-Severn Waterway. A boarding house and a school and many family houses lined Highway 507 at the place where a road led down to the river.

Highway 507 began when the government attempted to build a road north from Buckhorn in 1865. It took one year to push the Government Road six miles, another 15 years to reach beyond Catchacoma. A hundred years later the road was still notorious; as late as the 1970s, the Ontario road map bore a special notation warning that you used Highway 507 at your own risk.

Cottagers who built on Mississauga or Gold or Catchacoma in the 1960s and '70s, or ventured deeper into the wilderness of Cavendish and Galway, clearly remember the bumps and hairpin turns and heart-stopping surprises of Highway 507.

Today the highway is smooth but you still turn and twist over the rocks. This is still a harsh land but a beautiful one. A land with a sense of adventure and space for another day.

September tranquillity on the lake.

White birch

Shaggy Mane mushrooms appear like magic on a cottage road.

St. Peter's on-the-Rock has been summer church to generations of Stoney Lake cottagers.

Heritage canoes proudly owned by cottagers on Stoney Lake are tied up at St. Peter's during a 75th anniversary service in 1989.

Canoe race at Youngs Point.

Launching the boat is a spring event
throughout the Kawarthas.

Kayaker at Burleigh Falls.

Two suns appear in the morning mist which joins sky and water.

93

"My own boat."

Fishing from the dock.

The water ski landing.

Sailboarding on Big Cedar.

Cardinal flowers bloom along Burleigh Township creek.

Catharine Parr Traill, best known for her *Backwoods of Canada*, studied and collected plants and wrote *Canadian Wildflowers* (1868), followed by *Studies of Plant Life in Canada* (1885). Then, in her nineties, she wrote *Pearls and Pebbles or Notes of an Old Naturalist*. She first saw the Cardinal Flower on her journey up the Otonabee in 1832.

It was but a short time before that I had seen it cultivated as a new and rare border flower, and here it was in all its loveliness on the banks of a lonely forest stream which then flowed through an almost unbroken wilderness ...

Catharine Parr Traill, *Studies of Plant Life in Canada*, 1885[1]

At the water's edge.

July weekend on Big Cedar.

Swimming with Mommy.

Skiers cross a lake.

Trails maintained by the Kawartha Nordic Ski Club run from Haultain into the Crown Game Preserve east of Highway 28.

This massive building recalls the time when Lindsay's industry crowded along the Scugog. Known as the Old Northern Casket place, it now houses the Canadian Pyjama & Shirt Company.

CHAPTER 8

LINDSAY COUNTRY
(OPS, EMILY, VERULAM, FENELON, MARIPOSA AND ELDON)

The wide main street of Lindsay is busy any day of the week. The street is wide because a fire in 1861 wiped out the centre of town. Four hotels, the grist and saw mills, the railway station, post office, and 83 other buildings were burned. Four hundred people were left homeless. A year later the town was unrecognizable. Instead of the narrow street that had been hacked out of the bush in the 1840s and lined with wooden buildings, Lindsay now had an enormously wide street with three-story brick buildings and a look of pride and prosperity much ahead of its time.

The town today is busy because it serves a rich farmland and a bustling cottage country. South of the lakes – Sturgeon, Cameron and Balsam – a limestone base is covered with clay loam which becomes deeper and richer as you move south. The township of Ops, with its Scugog River connecting Sturgeon Lake in the north to Scugog Lake in the south, is aptly named after the Roman goddess of plenty and fertility.

Mariposa to the west is even richer in soil but early settlement was hampered by poor drainage. Along with its swampy character went the fear of ague. A further slowdown was caused by land speculation. Watson Kirkconnell in his history of Victoria County says, *George Strange Boulton of Port Hope, the Family Compact member for Durham, arranged a rich grant to himself, and lesser octopuses were not wanting.*[1]

Verulam township is divided by the east arm of Sturgeon Lake into northern and southern portions. At the eastern end of the arm, two river channels lead to Pigeon Lake. Champlain in 1615, referred to this place as Beaubocage (beautiful grove of trees). In early days a trader named Billy McDeough (McCue) set up shop at this spot to trade with Indians in the area. Today the village of Bobcaygeon enjoys the scenery of its two rivers and the boats locking through on the Trent Severn Waterway.

Finished stooking.

Fenelon township, with most of Sturgeon Lake, all of Cameron Lake and South Bay of Balsam Lake within its boundaries, is about equal parts land and water. At the top arm of Sturgeon Lake, the village of Fenelon Falls has Cameron Lake on its west side, its water dropping 7 m over a cliff, then tumbling through the short Fenelon River down to Sturgeon Lake. All early travellers raved about the beauty of the falls here in the forest, comparable they said to the beauty of Niagara.

Eldon township has the distinction of having the 'other' hydraulic lift lock. The 14.5 m Kirkfield Lift Lock, with its framework of open-web steel, differs in appearance from the concrete Peterborough Lift Lock. Opened in 1907, three years after the Peterborough one, it remains an engineering wonder which delights the boaters who use it, and attracts visitors by road to this height of land where the Kawartha Lakes begin.

Reflections on the Scugog River.

Fishing by Lock 33 in Lindsay.

Boats locking through at Fenelon Falls.

Opposite: Horses at Lindsay fair.

Wolves pause on a melting pond in early spring.

The usual cry of the wolf is a long, smooth howl. It is quite musical, though decidedly eerie when heard in the woods at night. I cannot distinguish it from the howl of a large dog. Its beginning is also much like the hoot of an owl. This is usually the "muster" or "rallying cry" – the intimation of the wolf to his friends that he has found game too strong for him to manage alone. It is the call commonly heard at night about the settlers' cabins and it never fails to affect me personally with a peculiar prickling in the scalp that I doubt not is a racial inheritance from the Stone Age.

Ernest Thompson Seton, *Lives of Game Animals, 1953.*[2]

Ernest Thompson was six years old when he came to Lindsay. The Thompsons, with 10 sons and one daughter, settled on a farm in the forest east of Lindsay. It was here that Ernest discovered wild living things and his own self-reliance.

The family failed at bush farming and moved to Toronto when Ernest was 10. But when he became ill at 15, his mother guessed that the old farm might help. Friends named Blackwell owned it now and she sent Ernest to them.

Young Sam Blackwell became the friend that thousands of readers know in *Two Little Savages*. William Blackwell became the rugged, gentle father Ernest needed, a contrast to his own father who was stern and sometimes cruel. A neighbour named Caleb Clark taught the boys how to build a wigwam and showed them the tricks and skills of woodcraft. A woman, known as the Lindsay Witch, also shared natural wisdom and secrets with them.

Partly in rebellion against his father, Ernest changed his name to Seton, the name of a Scottish ancestor. After he won a gold medal in the Ontario Art School he went to London to study, almost starving while there. His need for wilderness and his need for the artistic recognition he could get only in the city, bounced him back and forth: to his brother's homestead in Manitoba, to New York to sell his art and writing, back to Manitoba, where he became official naturalist to the government, to Toronto, to a farm at Port Credit, to Paris to study art.

As naturalist, artist, author and storyteller, he travelled all over Canada and the United States, studying the world of animals, passing on his knowledge in more than 40 books, hundreds of articles and 3000 lectures. He brought the Boy Scout movement to America and served as its chief from 1910 to 1915.

Wolves were of special interest to Seton. His mother had named him Ernest Evan after a great Scottish hunter said to have killed the last wolf in Scotland with his bare hands. His paintings of wolves, particularly *The Sleeping Wolf* and the controversial *Triumph of the Wolves* were among his best. He sometimes used a wolf print as part of his signature.

He died at Santa Fe, New Mexico, where he and his second wife, Julia, built their dream castle. But a little community called Reaboro near Lindsay remembers that this great man of the out-of-doors discovered wild living things and his own self-reliance here when he was a boy.

Eastern Bluebird on fence post.

Then, in March came a definite thaw. The sky was brilliantly blue that day; and, about nine o'clock, a little bird warbled softly in a lone poplar by the house. One of the older boys said it was a bluebird. I thought I could see its blue back. Again and again it sang its simple notes. It made me cry; I don't know why; but I loved it. It has been my spring bird ever since.

Ernest Thompson Seton, *Trail of an Artist-Naturalist, 1951.[3]*

This grand willow is a signature tree at the Fenlon Falls park.

Apple tree and shingled shed near Cameron on highway 35

This massive Boyd barn near Bobcaygeon recalls the Boyd family's lumber empire and M.M. Boyd's interest in cattle breeding. His Double Standard Polled Herefords gained fame around the world.

On Big Island in Pigeon Lake, M.M. Boyd cross-bred buffalo and cattle to produce "cattalo". Buffalo and "cattalo" are still found on several Kawartha farms.

A harvest of hay bales and a stormy sky promise winter weather.

Old mill at Norland evokes the mood of days when lumber sang on the saws and massive log drives moved down the Gull River into Shadow Lake.

CHAPTER 9

WILD LANDS BEYOND
(VERULAM, SOMERVILLE, BEXLEY, CARDEN, DIGBY, DALTON AND LONGFORD)

Early writers discussing the upper Kawartha Lakes referred to the land above the lakes as "the wild lands beyond". Settlement came late to the region, partly because of distance, and partly because the soil on top of the glaciated limestone or metamorphic rock was "thin and uncertain".

The country was wild in several senses. A ride on the so-called roads that wandered north from Bobcaygeon or Fenelon Falls or Rosedale or Coboconk was invariably described as a wild and bone-wrenching experience. A man, who had driven a stage coach on the Cariboo Trail in the mountains of British Columbia, declared the worst road in Canada to be the Bobcaygeon Road.

George S. Thompson coming up the Great Bobcaygeon Road in 1869 feared his *"toenails would be shaken off that first trip of mine."*[1] A. Parsonage said, if any road *"was ever made purposely to upset the passengers the Bobcaygeon must be the one."*[2]

Many of the people going into the country were a wild lot themselves, tough foremen and river bosses working for hard-driving lumber barons like Boyd, Carew, Rathburn, Gilmour, McDonald or Dickson. In the late 1800s taverns existed every few miles along the Great Bobcaygeon Road and were well used. In Bobcaygeon, storekeeper Irvine Junkin was concerned for the women and children who often went hungry after the lumbermen's wages were wasted on liquor at the Rockland House or the Rokeby Hotel. When he started a temperance movement in the 1880s his store and attached home were set on fire; he and his family barely escaped.

Names on the map of Victoria County's northern townships tell only half the story. Corson's Siding on the northwest shore of Balsam was known for years as Hell's Half Acre. Gooderham & Worts, Toronto distillers, owned a large timber limit near this little railway village where they cut timber for cordwood.

*Tamarack and rail fences on a limestone plain typical of the
limestone outcrops which appear north of the lakes.*

They would send up a lake captain, named Corson, as foreman of the winter cut. Sailors, collected in Toronto, made up his timber gang. With them went unlimited quantities of whisky and a collection of prostitutes. The site was soon infamous throughout the north and until the timber ran out near the end of the century, it was known as Hell's Half acre.

The country itself was wild – thousands of acres of forest, white pine, maple and beech, stretching into the Haliburton Highlands, which consisted of more thousands of acres of forest. It was a land abundant with game and it had streams teeming with fish, at least until the lumbermen slashed and burned and laid it to waste. Tales are told of 5000 muskies speared at Coboconk in one year.

The fast streams made it easy to move vast quantities of timber down to the lakes. Giant pines were floated on to Quebec. Smaller timber was sawn at the mills established on the rivers or where the rivers met lakes or where one lake spilled into another.

Apart from the army of men cutting trees, there were families at work at depot farms like the one on Nogie's Creek or like Uphill (a depot for the Longford Lumber Company), there were men cadging supplies into the camps, teamsters hauling timbers to the water, rivermen moving logs downstream and work crews building and repairing dams and timber slides.

The slide at Norland was 6.9 m long and 11 m wide, big enough to let a crib of square timber move down or let a raft holding the cook's shanty and all the sleeping quarter equipment take the plunge. In 1884 the Boyd firm put 50 000 logs over the Norland slide. With the timber from all the other companies, an estimated 200 000 to 300 000 logs were moving down the Gull River. A few miles to the east in Somerville township, similar log drives were moving down to Cameron Lake.

Dams and slides took a terrible beating. Log jams would sometimes tear away whole sections of the slides. Crews worked to rebuild cribwork and sluice-ways, replace stop-logs and repair windlasses, refloor the slides with hemlock planks, fix the guide booms and mend the piers to which they were anchored.

Lumbering was a hit-and-run operation although the hit lasted almost a century. Bereft of its trees, the land had a few pockets of fertility where the logger-turned-farmer could raise a family. But most areas which had been covered by park-like forests now revealed bare rock. Forest fires finished the destruction, actually removing the thin layer of humus. It is not surprising that these northern townships had a mass exodus of lumbering families who headed for the West near the end of the century.

In this century the forest struggles to re-establish itself. Since 1928 the Victoria County Forest, a joint project of the county and the Ministry of Natural Resources, has put millions of young trees on the land. With a little help from such friends, the wilderness which fed the lumberman and frustrated the farmer now attracts the tourist, the sportsman, the cottager. Here is a land of rivers and lakes, of rocks and second-growth forest holding on to the natural beauty and wildness craved by those who must live most of their lives in cities to the south of the lakes.

If I cou'd see the daisy spread
Its wee flowers owre the lee;
Or the heather scent the mountain breeze,
And the ivy climb the tree;
If I cou'd see the lane kirk yard,
Whar' frien's lie side by side:
And think that I cou'd lay my banes
Beside them when I died:
Then might I think this forest hame,
And in it live and dee;
Nor feel regret at my heart's core
My native land, for thee.

Verses from *My Hame.*[3]

The poem, *My Hame*, was published in the Cobourg Star in 1831. It was probably written by Thomas Carr who settled near Rice Lake on land which became the village of Keene. But the longing for home was experienced in every Kawartha township as settlers moved north throughout the area and pioneers tried to forget their "ould country" and make this forest home.

A "forest home" north of the lakes.

Resort near Rosedale.

St. John's Anglican Church at Rosedale.
(July and August Only)
ENTER REST PRAY

Cottage toys.

*The Gordon Boat Harbour has catered to the needs of boaters since
Dr. Thorne started a canoe factory here before the turn of the century.*

Stan and Don Nichols prepare a beaver pelt in Bobcaygeon.

Ducks enjoy the winter sun at Coboconk.

Farmhouse near Burnt River

*Flooding and freezing has formed tables of
shimmering ice throughout a swamp.*

Lake fog in October.

This morning was beautiful; it was just freezing but no more and there was a fog over the lake. These lake fogs are sometimes exceedingly picturesque, rolling up or down the lake with the wind.

Anne Langton, October 15, 1838.[4]

In letters to her brother William in England, Anne Langton described life on Sturgeon Lake in the 1830s and 1840s. She was 33 years old when she, her father, mother and Aunt Alice followed her brother John to Canada to live on the upper arm of Sturgeon Lake. She managed a large household, working under difficult conditions to maintain the social niceties of the English upper class.

Anne became the area's first school teacher. She also found time to sketch the changing scene of her backwoods life. In *A Gentlewoman in Upper Canada*, edited by H.H. Langton, we can read her letters home and see the mists move over the lake through the eyes of a newcomer and an artist.

Fishing from the shore at Bobcaygeon.

Canoe in morning mist.

NOTES

Chapter 1

1. Green, Anson, D.D., *Life and Times of Anson Green*, D.D. (Toronto: Methodist Book Room, 1877) 56.

Chapter 2

1. Ryerson, Rev. Egerton, "*The Story of My Life*" (Toronto: William Briggs, 1883) 74.

2. Kah-ge-ga-gah-bowh (Copway, George), *Traditional History and Characteristic Sketches of the Ojibway Nation* (Boston: Benjamin Mussey & Co., 1851) xi.

3. Bonnycastle, Sir Richard, *Canada and the Canadians in 1846,* 2 vols. (London, 1849) 240-242.

Chapter 3

1. Laurence, Margaret, *Heart of a Stranger* (Toronto: McClelland & Stewart, 1976) 188-189.

2 Laurence, Margaret, *Dance on the Earth, A Memoir* (Toronto: McClelland & Stewart, 1989) 200.

Chapter 4

1. Strickland, Sam, *Twenty-Seven Years in Canada West*, 2 vols. (London: Richard Bentley, 1853) 237.

Chapter 5

1. Moodie, J.W.D., *Scenes and Adventures, as a Soldier and Settler, during Half a Century* (Montreal, 1866) 219-29, from Guillet, E.C. Valley of the Trent (Toronto: The Champlain Society, 1957) 395-399.

2. Fowke, Edith, *Traditional Singers and Songs from Ontario* (Don Mills: Burns and MacEachern Ltd., 1965) 1.

3. Peterborough Centennial Museum Archives

4. Traill, Catharine Parr, *The Backwoods of Canada* (Toronto: McClelland & Stewart, 1929) 70-71.

5. Fowke 3.

Chapter 6

1. Watson, Robert T., *The Broken Twig* (Madoc Printing & Publishing, 1990) 42.

2. Guillet, E.C., *The Valley of the Trent* (Toronto: The Champlain Society, 1957) 25.

3. Buell diaries, loaned by Connie Wahl.

Chapter 7

1. Cummings, H.R., *Early Days in Haliburton* (Department of Lands and Forests, 1963) 52.

Chapter 8

1. Kirkconnell, Watson, *County of Victoria Centennial History* (Victoria County Council, 1921) 22.

2. Seton, E.T., *Lives of Game Animals* (Boston: Charles T. Branford, Company, 1953) 283

3. Seton, E.T., *Trail of an Artist-Naturalist* (London: Hodder and Stoughton) 39.

Chapter 9

1. Cummings, 38

2. Cummings 38.

3. Guillet 428.

4. Langton, Anne, *A Gentlewoman in Upper Canada* (Toronto: Clarke, Irwin, 1950) 74.

BIBLIOGRAPHY

Adams, Peter and Taylor, Colin, *Peterborough and the Kawarthas* (Heritage Publications, 1985).

Bonnycastle, Sir Richard, *Canada and the Canadians in 1846*, 2 Vols. (London, 1849).

Bowley, Robert E., *Connections between the names Pengelley, Brock, Roche & Scriven in Monaghan Township* (Peterborough: R. Bowley, 1993).

Boyce, G.E., *Eldorado* (Toronto: Natural Heritage-Natural History, 1992).

Brown, Lorraine, The Trent-Severn Waterway: an Environmental Exploration (Peterborough: Friends of the Trent-Severn Waterway, 1994).

Brunger, Alan G., *Harvey Township* (The Greater Harvey Historical Society, 1992).

Carr, Mrs. Ross N., *Ops, Land of Plenty* (Ops Historical Committee, 1968).

Carr, Violet M., *The Rolling Hills* (Manvers Township Council, 1967).

Cole, Jean Murray, *The Loon Calls* (Township of Chandos, 1989).

Cole, Jean Murray, *Origins – The History of Dummer Township* (Township of Dummer, 1993).

Cole, A.O.C. and Cole, Jean M. (eds.), *Kawartha Heritage* (Peterborough Historical Atlas Foundation, 1981).

Cummings, H.R., *Early Days in Haliburton* (Department of Lands and Forests, 1963).

Edmison, J. Alex (ed.), *Through the Years in Douro* (Township of Douro, 1968).

Frost, Leslie M., *Forgotten Pathways of the Trent* (Don Mills: Burns & MacEachern, 1973).

Fowke, Edith, *Traditional Singers and Songs from Ontario* (Don Mills: Burns and MacEachern, 1965).

Galvin, Clare F., *The Holy Land* (Corporation of the Township of Ennismore, 1978).

Graham, Jean Lancaster, *Asphodel* (Township of Asphodel, 1978).

Green, Anson, *The Life and Times of the Rev. Anson Green*, D.D., (Toronto: Methodist Book Room, 1877).

Guillet, E.C., *The Valley of the Trent* (Toronto: The Champlain Society, 1957).

Hewitt, D.F., *Geology and Scenery Peterborough, Bancroft and Madoc Area* (Ministry of Natural Resources, 1969).

Hooke, Katharine, *St. Peter's On-The-Rock* (75th Anniversary Committee, 1989).

Jones, Elwood and Dyer, Bruce, *Peterborough The Electric City* (Windsor Publications, 1987).

Kah-ge-ga-gah-bowh (Copway, George), *Traditional History and Characteristic Sketches of the Ojibway Nation* (Boston: Benjamin Mussey & Co., 1851).

Kirkconnell, Watson, *County of Victoria Centennial History (Lindsay, 1967)*.

Langton, H.H. (ed.), *Early Days in Upper Canada* (Toronto: Clarke Irwin, 1950).

Laurence, Margaret, *Dance on the Earth*, A Memoir (Toronto: McClelland & Stewart, 1989).

Laurence, Margaret, *Heart of a Stranger* (Toronto: McClelland & Stewart, 1976).

LeCrae R.V., *The Land Between* (The Residents of Laxton, Dighby & Longford, 1967).

Mallory, Enid, Coppermine *The Far North of George M. Douglas* (Peterborough: Broadview Press, 1989, distribution: Peterborough Publishing).

Mallory, Enid, *Kawartha: Living on These Lakes* (Peterborough Publishing, 1991).

Martin, Norma, and Milne, Catharine, and McGillis, Donna, *Gore's Landing and the Rice Lake Plains* (Heritage Gore's Landing, 1986).

Moodie, Susanna, *Roughing it in the Bush*, 2 Vols. (London: Richard Bentley, 1852).

Nelson, D.G., *From Forest to Farm* (Keene: Otonabee 150th Anniversary Committee, 1975).

Pammett, Howard T., *Lilies and Shamrocks* (Municipality of Emily, 1974).

Philpot, Andre L., *A Species of Adventure* (Marmora: Irontown Publications, 1990)

Ryerson, Rev. Egerton, *"The Story of My Life"* (Toronto: William Briggs, 1883).

Seton, Ernest Thompson, *Lives of Game Animals*, (Boston: Charles R. Branford Company, 1953).

Stewart, Frances, *Our Forest Home* (Montreal: Gazette Publishing, 1902).

Strickland, Samuel, C.M., Twenty-Seven Years in Canada West (London: Richard Bentley, 1853).

Suggit, Gladys, *Roses and Thorns* (Fenelon Falls: John Deyell, 1972).

Theberge, Clifford and Elaine, At the Edge of the Shield (Smith Township Historical Committee, 1982).

Thomas, W.D., *Bobcaygeon The Hub of the Kawarthas* (Bobcaygeon: John Deyell, 1980).

Thompson, George S., *Up to Date or The Life of a Lumberman* (Peterboro: Times Print, 1895).

Traill, Catharine Parr, *The Backwoods of Canada* (London: Charles Knight, 1836).

Watson, Robert T., *The Broken Twig* (Madoc Printing & Publishing, 1990).

Whetung-Derrick, Mae, *History of Ojibway of the the Curve Lake Reserve* (Curve Lake Indian Band #35, 1976).

Whitfield, Alta, *A History of North Monaghan Township 1817-1989* (North Monaghan Township, 1989).